Fear Forest

Steve Cole • Jonatronix

Westmeads Community Infant School
Cromwell Road
Whitstable
Kent
CT5 1NA
Tel: 01227 272995
Fax: 01227 280459
headteacher@westmeads.kent.sch.uk

OXFORD
UNIVERSITY PRESS

Max's mission log

We are travelling through space on board the micro-ship Excelsa with our new friends, Nok and Seven.

We're on a mission to save Planet Exis (Nok's home planet), which is running out of power. We need to collect four fragments that have been hidden throughout the Beta-Prime Galaxy. Together the fragments form the Core of Exis. Only the Core will restore power to the planet.

It's not easy. A space villain called Badlaw wants the power of the Core for himself. His army of robotic Krools is never far behind us!

Fragments collected so far: 2

Current location: Planet Kree-Marr

In our last adventure …

A jamming device had made our ship crash and stopped our watches from working. We were stuck at micro-size!

We split up. Ant, Tiger and Seven went to find the jammer. They found a spaceship graveyard … and some scary creatures called Meebs. They also had to escape some Krools!

Meanwhile, Cat, Nok and I went to look for the fragment …

Chapter 1 – Forest explorers

Micro-sized Max, Cat and Nok were searching for the fragment. They walked across the dried-up swamp and eventually reached the edge of a forest.

"The fragment is in there somewhere," said Nok. "At least, I think it is. The energy coming from it is very weak."

Carefully they made their way into the forest. Eerie purple trees stretched over their heads. Their bare branches made the trees look dead. Everything looked parched.

"I hope the others can stop the jammer," Cat said. She checked her watch. It was not working, which meant they were all still stuck at micro-size.

Cat heard a rustling noise behind her. She spun round.

There was no one there – just two big, beautiful flowers. They had white petals that drooped down and purple twisting roots.

"I don't remember passing those," said Cat.

Max, Cat and Nok continued on through the sickly-looking forest. They saw more of the white flowers peeping out from behind the trees.

"I have a funny feeling we're being watched," murmured Max.

Then the friends heard sinister, squelching, sucking sounds just ahead of them.

"Feed … Mmmmm … Feed …"

Through the reeds, they saw a swarm of large, blue jellyfish-creatures floating in a shallow pool of green goo.

"It's the creatures we met before," said Nok. "Meebs!"

Chapter 2 – Mobbed by Meebs

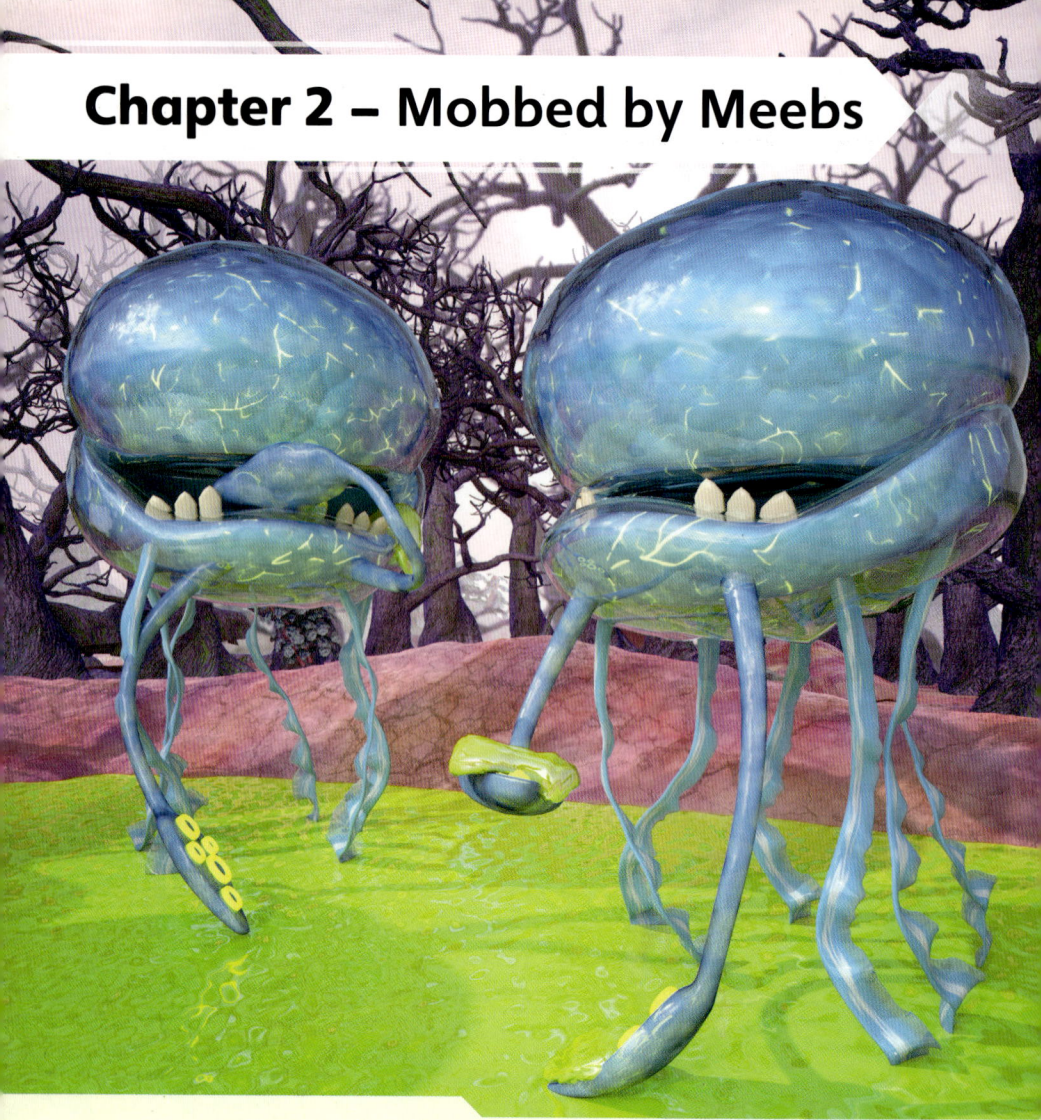

"Ugh," said Cat, watching as the Meebs gulped down the goo. "All those creatures seem to think about is food."

Then one Meeb looked their way. "Alert!" it hissed. "Small animals sighted!"

The swarm rose up angrily into the air and whipped their tentacles towards the micro-friends. "Food is ours," came the eerie cries. "Not share! Ours!"

"Time for a quick getaway," said Max.

The three friends hurried back through the forest. The path was crowded with more of the tall white flowers.

"I'm sure they weren't all here before," said Cat.

"Never mind that now, they will make a perfect hiding place," Max said, panting. "We can climb inside the flowers and wait until the Meebs have gone past!"

Max, Nok and Cat each chose a different flower and climbed up. They wriggled between the smooth petals. Inside, the flowers smelled sickly sweet.

Moments later, the angry Meebs stopped in front of the flowers. They looked around and flicked their tentacles to and fro. "Small ones gone," they muttered. "Us never share food!" Then they turned and bobbed back the way they had come.

"Phew," thought Max. "They've gone." He tried to climb back out of the big, white flower, but the petals closed around him. "Hey! I can't get out!" he shouted.

"Nor can I!" yelled Cat.

Nok pushed against the petals. "I'm trapped too!"

"Do not struggle," came a gurgling voice. "You are our prisoners!"

"Talking flowers?" Max spluttered.

"*Starving* flowers!" The three plants shook and shivered. "We are the Gubloons, and this is our forest. Since the Meebs started drinking all our sap, intruders are NOT welcome!"

Chapter 3 – Flower power

"Let us go!" cried Nok.

"Silence, intruders," hissed the Gubloon. "We shall take you to our leader, Necktor. She will choose your fate." The three plants suddenly lurched forward on rooty legs.

"*These things can walk!*" thought Cat. "So that's *how they seemed to spring up from nowhere.*"

Gubloons

Information

Gubloons are plants that can walk and talk. There are different types of Gubloons. You can tell them apart by their different coloured flowers. The most common are white Gubloons.

Diet
Gubloons feed on the sap of Kree-Marr.

Habitat
Gubloons are found mainly in the forests of Kree-Marr.

large petals

mouth

moveable roots

Necktor

Necktor is a big, yellow Gubloon. She is the oldest flower on the planet and is the leader of all the other Gubloons.

The Gubloons took their terrified prisoners through the forest and up a steep hill.

"Great Necktor," called one of the Gubloons. "We bring you three strange fleshy-things."

Through the gaps in the petals, Max could see that Necktor was a big, yellow Gubloon. She overlooked the forest below from a small puddle of thick, green sap.

Necktor's leaves quivered. "Bring them closer. Let me look upon them …"

The Gubloons bent down close to the ground and opened their petal mouths. As they did so, Cat looked down at her watch.

"The power's back!" she said. "Ant, Tiger and Seven must have stopped the jamming device!"

"You want to see us, Necktor? No problem!" Max pressed his button.

The next moment, he returned to normal size. He was quickly followed by Cat and Nok. The Gubloons screamed and swayed in panic. Only Necktor remained calm.

"Greetings," Necktor said. "Hunger has made us mistrust strangers. I am sorry."

"That's OK." Cat felt sorry for the plants. At the bottom of the hill, she could see a swarm of Meebs. "The Meebs are drinking all your sap, aren't they? That's why the forest is dying."

"Our whole world is dying," Necktor sighed. "Little sap remains."

Nok pulled a bottle from his belt and walked over to the thick, gooey puddle. "I wonder …"

Chapter 4 – Unexpected help

"What is in that bottle?" asked Necktor.

"Water," Nok explained. "It's what we drink. There isn't much, but perhaps it will dilute your sap to make it last longer."

Cat's eyes lit up. "Like adding water to orange squash," she said. "Good idea, Nok!"

"Try," Necktor urged them. "Please, try."

Quickly, Max, Cat and Nok emptied their water bottles into the puddle, which grew a little bigger. Necktor shivered with joy. The other Gubloons each dipped in their roots. "Nice!" they sang.

"Uh, oh. I see something that's *not* so nice." Nok pointed down the hill. Six robotic shapes were rolling through the forest.

"Krools!" Cat groaned. "Badlaw's sent his army after us again."

"Right now, maybe the Krools can help us ..." said Max.

Max jumped up and down, waving his arms. "Hey, Krools! We're up here. Catch us if you can!"

Hearing Max's voice echo down the hillside, the Krools started rolling towards them.

Nok frowned. "Why did you do that?"

"You'll see," said Max.

29

To reach Necktor's hill, the Krools had to pass through the feeding Meebs.

The Meebs hissed at the sight of the robots. "Stay away! Sap is ours!"

The Krools ignored them. Instead they bowled the Meebs out of the way. Soon the jellyfish-monsters were in full retreat.

"The Meebs have been driven away!" sang Necktor.

"What about the Krools?" asked Cat. "They're coming for us!"

"You have helped us," said Necktor. "Now we will help you."

Necktor raised a leafy arm and pointed to a tiny tunnel in the hillside. "If you can make yourselves small again ... you can go in there," she suggested.

"I can feel the fragment more clearly now," said Nok. "It must be underground."

"Let's shrink," said Max. "We must find that fragment before the Krools do – whatever it takes!"

Find out what happens next in *Attack of the Giant Meeb.*